The Silence of Calvary

Meditations on
GOOD FRIDAY

The Silence of Calvary

Meditations on GOOD FRIDAY

Christopher L. Webber

Morehouse Publishing
NEW YORK

Morehouse Publishing, 19 East 34th Street, New York, NY 10016
Morehouse Publishing is an imprint of Church Publishing Incorporated.

Cover design by Jennifer Kopec, 2Pug Design
Typeset by Rose Design

Library of Congress Cataloging-in-Publication Data

Names: Webber, Christopher L., author.
Title: The silence of Calvary : meditations on Good Friday / Christopher L.
   Webber.
Description: New York, NY : Morehouse Publishing, [2021]
Identifiers: LCCN 2021032798 (print) | LCCN 2021032799 (ebook) |
   ISBN 9781640654709 (paperback) | ISBN 9781640654716 (epub)
Subjects: LCSH: Jesus Christ--Crucifixion--Meditations. | Good Friday--
   Meditations. | Silence--Religious aspects--Christianity--Meditations.
Classification: LCC BT453 .W35 2021 (print) | LCC BT453 (ebook) |
   DDC 232.96/3--dc23
LC record available at https://lccn.loc.gov/2021032798
LC ebook record available at https://lccn.loc.gov/2021032799

CONTENTS

PROLOGUE / vii

I
THE SILENCE OF CALVARY / 1

II
THE SILENCE OF THE PEOPLE / 15

III
THE SILENCE OF THE DISCIPLES / 27

IV
THE SILENCE OF MARY / 39

V
THE SILENCE OF JESUS / 53

VI
THE SILENCE OF GOD / 67

VII
THE SILENCE OF THE TOMB / 79

PROLOGUE

THERE'S A FAMILIAR NINETEENTH-CENTURY HYMN that makes an interesting point about Good Friday:

Sev'n times he spake, sev'n words of love;
    And all three hours his silence cried
For mercy on the souls of men;
    Jesus, our Lord, is crucified.[1]

Good Friday sermons and meditations have centered our attention again and again on the words Jesus spoke from the cross, but those few, brief words would have needed only a few minutes on the first Good Friday. Most of the time that Friday there was silence—a silence that speaks more loudly than words. The cross,

---

1. "O Come and Mourn with Me a While," *The Hymnal 1940* (New York: Church Pension Fund, 1940), hymn 74.

the most familiar symbol of the Christian faith, and the crucifix displayed in many churches and homes, still speak silently. No spoken words are needed to convey the message. Perhaps, then, it would be useful to think about that silence, the silence of Calvary. These brief meditations are designed to call attention to that silence that spoke once and that speaks still more loudly than many words.

✝

CHAPTER I

THE SILENCE
OF CALVARY

THERE IS, THE BIBLE SAYS, "a time to keep silence, and a time to speak" (Eccles. 3:7). Sometimes we know well enough what time it is, but sometimes we find it almost impossible to tell what time it is and what we ought to be doing. Good Friday is such a time.

Good Friday is unlike any other day of the year. We come to Good Friday midway between the triumphal entry of Palm Sunday and the joy of Easter. Here, between those joyous occasions, we stand before the cross, seeing Jesus nailed there, and for the moment we may almost forget what has gone before and what will come after.

What should we do on a day like this? What should our part be in this awful and glorious event? The history of the church gives no clear answer. Some have believed that this is a day above all days to receive communion. Is it not, after all, on the cross that the body of Christ is broken for us and the blood of Christ poured out? And doesn't Paul say that "as often as you eat this bread and drink the cup, you proclaim the Lord's death until he comes"? (1 Cor. 11:26). In some churches that has been the tradition, and there is good precedent for it.

But some would say, "No." Some would say that this is the time above all times *not* to celebrate the Eucharist or receive communion. Some would say that that great feast, that victory celebration of the people of

God, cannot take place on this day. They would say that it is the risen body of Christ that we receive in the Eucharist, and to do that on this day is to put the wrong meaning on this day and on the Eucharist as well. The victory is not complete until Easter; there should be no celebration till then. And there is good precedent for that tradition also.

For many years it has also been the custom in some churches to preach during the three hours from noon to mid-afternoon on the words of Christ from the cross. Often it has been an opportunity for various churches to come together ecumenically in a way they cannot do ordinarily, but that custom is, I think, slowly dying out. Perhaps we are so overwhelmed with words coming at us from all our electronic devices that the thought of more words has less appeal than it once did. So the Book of Common Prayer, beginning on page 276, provides alternative forms of prayer for Good Friday and suggested readings for this time and many churches use them.

But one thing seems clear: that on this day we should do nothing, say nothing, think nothing, except of the love of Jesus that is shown here on the cross. Any form of service, any prayers or hymns, that will keep our hearts and minds on that center can help us keep this day as followers of Christ and enter with him into the suffering and death from which come victory over all the power of evil.

"There is a time to keep silence," the Bible tells us, "and a time to speak." This is a time for silence.

If we are not sure what to do on Good Friday, it is at least in part because there is nothing we can do. All that can be done is being done, there on the cross. Our role is to be silent observers as Jesus acts for us. And let us remember this: our silence is a mixture of many elements. There is sorrow of course, and a sense of awe and wonder, but never forget that there is also joy even on this day because this is not a time of defeat or failure. What we are watching is a victory being won and being won for us.

This is *Good* Friday, God's Friday, a day of victory, and our role is first of all as observers: to see and understand as far as we can the suffering and death by which that victory is won.

This is a time for silence. This is a time for the concentration of all our hearts and minds on the cross of Christ and the thing that is happening there for our salvation.

The usual Good Friday meditations ask us to ponder Jesus's words from the cross, and that is surely valuable. But those words were few and brief and surrounded by silence. What if, then, we centered our thoughts, not on the traditional words from the cross, but on the silences. The purpose is the same: to provide a focal point for our thoughts and prayers, to assist us, to guide us, because finally each of us has to play our own part, make our own offering, place ourselves there with Christ, take part with him in his suffering and share in his death in order to share in his victory.

These words then are simply guideposts for us to follow and we will need to add to them our own offering of penitence and prayer and praise. The most important part is to find time for silence, because in the silence most of all, we can become not only witnesses, but also participants in this event.

We might begin by placing ourselves in the city of Jerusalem on that first Good Friday. That was not a silent place, at least at first. The city was filled with noise, and the noise was not only that of an important city going about its day's work, but the noise and confusion of the throngs that had come from all over the world to keep the Passover, the great traditional feast of the Jewish people.

There were Jews in Jerusalem who had never have been in Jerusalem before, and who hardly spoke the same language as Jews from other parts of the Roman Empire; there were travelers seeking a place to stay; there were businessmen working to set their affairs in order before the holiday began; there were housewives preparing their homes and their meals for the celebration. Picture Times Square on New Year's Eve, a department store three days before Christmas, so Jerusalem would have been at that Passover time.

And this year there were other noises. This year someone had come who had drawn crowds after him, crowds of people shouting his praise. For most of the week they had followed him, watched him, listened to him, debated with him. But gradually the crowd's mood had changed: from praise and expectancy to watchfulness and questioning, and at last to doubt and disappointment. Gradually the crowds grew smaller.

But then larger crowds formed, and this time they formed in anger and hatred. Early in the morning the crowd nearly got out of control in the governor's courtyard. They had been whipped up and urged on to demand an execution. This man had failed them. He had rejected the use of force. He had done nothing to rid them of the Romans. He had not done what they wanted him to do, expected him to do.

Some had always considered him dangerous; now all of them were willing to join in shouting, "Let him be crucified." At last the governor had yielded to their demands. There had been the possibility of dangerous rioting. Barely in time to prevent it, the governor had agreed to the execution they wanted.

Still there was noise, but now it was the noise of the people on the way to enjoy the execution; now it was the shouts of the soldiers trying to keep them back and maintain order; now it was the jeers and the insults of those who had worked to see this crucifixion take place:

Hail, King of the Jews! (Mark 15:18)

You that destroy the temple and build it again in three days, save yourself. (Mark 15:29–30)

You who would destroy the temple and build it in three days, save yourself! If you are the Son of God, come down from the cross. (Matt. 27:40)

The rulers derided, the soldiers mocked, and the people stood watching.

The first blow of the hammers, the sharp sound of ringing metal, brought a moment's silence. This was what they had come to see and hear. So there was silence almost for the first time that day, and they could hear his words: "Father, forgive them; for they do not know what they are doing" (Luke 23:34).

For a moment there was silence, the kind of silence that falls on any crowd in moments of expectation, or when interest is failing and they wait for something new to take place.

It would happen again and again in the course of that long afternoon. The crowd grew smaller, the shouts and the jeers became fewer; there were even moments of silence, and from time to time those who stood nearest the cross would hear Jesus speak.

Seven times he spoke; seven words were remembered: words of love, words of suffering, words of triumph and victory. These, tradition recorded. Had the noise been less, had the silence been longer, would anyone have heard more? We have no way of knowing. People have often wished that the gospels were longer and more detailed, that more of Christ's words were recorded. There's always an audience for someone claiming to have uncovered new facts about Christ, new sayings of Jesus, new stories about him.

The search will still go on, of course, for writings that will tell us more, but no more is really needed. All that needs to be said, has been said. We already know all that we need to know. And if there is silence enough, if we will quietly wait on God, we will still hear him speak, because Jesus did not so much speak the word of God as reveal it, not so much by words as by actions, not so much in sayings and parables as in his life and by his life. He himself *is* God's word, made flesh so we might hear it. It is he himself and what he did for us that God wants us to know, for by him—by

his life and powerfully by his death—we know God
and hear God speak.

When he healed the crippled and blind, when he
raised the dead, when he forgave sin, when he fed
the hungry, it was what he did, not his words, that
spoke of God's healing love. So at Calvary it is the
pierced hands and side, the suffering and thirst, the
blood poured out, by which Jesus speaks God's word.
The wounds, the suffering, tell us God loves us, if we
will listen.

So it is silence that God asks of us on Good Friday,
silence and watchfulness, to stand beholding the love of
God and God's mercy. What we need to do is to silence
not only the sounds, but the hurry and clutter and wan-
dering thoughts, to silence every distraction as much as
we can, and listen, heart and mind and soul, to God's
incarnate word. The hymn says,

> Sev'n times he spake, sev'n words of love;
>> And all three hours his silence cried
> For mercy on the souls of men;
>> Jesus, our Lord, is crucified.

Over and over again God speaks God's word to
God's people, but how seldom there is silence enough
for us to hear. We would rather hear our own words.

We are hypnotized by the sound of our own voices. And so we fail to hear God speak.

Perhaps we comfort ourselves with the thought that if God really wanted us to hear, if God's command and our obedience were really important, God would compel our attention and make us hear. But the frightening truth is that God will not compel our attention. God has let God's love for us be nailed up on a signpost for the world to see, but if we choose to ignore it, the choice is ours to make.

God has given us freedom, and God will not take it away from us, not even to save our souls. All God asks is that we be silent and listen.

Was there ever a time when people were less willing to be silent than today? The people of Jesus's time in Palestine disliked his words; they tortured and crucified him to make him silent. But we seldom stop and keep silence to hear God's words in the first place. It seems as if we are afraid of silence, afraid of what we might hear.

Talk about the noise of Jerusalem that Good Friday and the noise of the crowd of Calvary! What about the noise of our own community or home any day of the week? Of course there are noises we can't control: the heavy trucks, the motors, the factories and machines. But there are other noises, too, that we might control, that keep us from having any silence whether for ourselves or for God. The television set: in how many houses is it ever turned off until something inside burns out? It stays on even when no one is in the room—or worse, when others are in the room, even when guests come to call. And the noise follows us out into the street: we see so many with ear buds in place or cell phones attached to their ears, so dependent on noise that they carry it with them. It's as if we were afraid that there might come a time when there was silence and we would be alone with our own thoughts, as if we were afraid of our own thoughts, or afraid of finding that the noise has killed them off and we don't have any thoughts.

But we come to the cross, we should come to the cross, for the sake of silence: to shut out the noise and confusion of everyday life, to quiet the voices of pleasure and pain, need and worry, family, business, and friends, and hear from the cross the word that is spoken there—often in silence more effectively than in words—the incarnate word of God.

The Old Testament emphasizes again and again the silence that is proper in God's presence:

The LORD is in his holy temple;
let all the earth keep silence before him! (Hab. 2:20)

Be silent, all people, before the LORD. (Zech. 2:13)

Perhaps you remember the story of Elijah the prophet. He went out into the wilderness seeking to hear God speak, and he listened for the voice of God in the wind and the thunder and the earthquake.

> Now there was a great wind, so strong that it was splitting mountains and breaking rocks in pieces before the LORD, but the LORD was not in the wind; and after the wind an earthquake, but the LORD was not in the earthquake; and after the earthquake a fire, but the LORD was not in the fire; and after the fire a sound of sheer silence. (1 Kings 19:11–12)

It could also be translated, "a thundering silence." It was in that thundering silence that God spoke.

Why is it that we so often fail to hear God speak? Is it because God speaks only occasionally, or only to those rare people we call prophets and saints? No, God wants us to hear. And if we do not hear, it may be that it is not because of God's silence, but because of our lack of silence, because we let ourselves be deafened by our own voices and sounds. These we must learn to silence to hear God.

We have familiar hymns that say the same thing:

> Jesus calls us o'er the tumult
> of our life's wild, restless sea,

Jesus calls us! By thy mercies,
Savior, may we hear thy call.[1]

Let all mortal flesh keep silence,
and with fear and trembling stand;
ponder nothing earthly minded,
for with blessing in his hand
Christ our God to earth descendeth,
our full homage to demand.[2]

Breathe through the heats of our desire
Thy coolness and thy balm
Let sense be dumb, let flesh retire
Speak through the earthquake, wind, and fire,
O still small voice of calm.[3]

Where hearts and minds are turned to him alone
there we will hear God speak.

Let us take for our subject and example the silence
of Calvary.

---

1. "Jesus Calls Us; O'er the Tumult," *The Hymnal 1982* (New York:
Church Hymnal, 1985), hymn 549.

2. "Let All Mortal Flesh Keep Silence," *The Hymnal 1982* (New
York: Church Hymnal, 1985), hymn 324.

3. "Dear Lord and Father of Mankind," *The Hymnal 1982* (New
York: Church Hymnal, 1985), hymn 653.

✝

CHAPTER II

THE SILENCE
OF THE PEOPLE

Holy Week begins with the tumult of Palm Sunday and reaches its climax with the tumult of Good Friday. The shouts and cheers that greeted Jesus on his entry into Jerusalem are matched by the shouts and jeers that follow him as he leaves the city carrying his cross. But gradually this crowd will melt away, because basically they don't care what happens. They have demanded his crucifixion for many reasons: some because their pride was hurt when Jesus seemed to reject their tribute, when it turned out he was not the messiah they had wanted; some because someone else had put them up to it in the first place; some because it seemed like the popular thing to do. But they have seen all they needed to see and have no reason to stay.

For any of these reasons and more they were willing to shout and demand his crucifixion. They will frighten Pilate into going against his better judgment. They will follow the soldiers out to the place of crucifixion. They will do all these things, but they will not stay to see what they have done.

Gradually the crowd will drift back to the city and their homes and businesses because at heart they do not care. It has been selfishness, pride, and indifference that have brought them to stand at the foot of the cross. But these motives will hardly hold them there on a busy day with the threat of a storm in the distance. There is little to hold them there during the long hours of suffering that show how much God loves them. They've had their way; they've gotten their wish; before the end comes, most have silently melted away.

Here God is speaking as never before in human history. Never again will the world be the same. But for most of the crowd it is just one more day, and long before it is finished they will be back in the city going about their business, indifferent still to what has taken place.

As this crowd dwindles away, the noise also lessens and the silence of Calvary grows. No silence is as cruel as this one. It is one thing to speak of our love and be rejected; it is another thing entirely to speak of our love and find that the one we love simply does not care. But that's how God's love for us is answered time and again. It's not that we disbelieve in God. We would not, for the most part, deny God's existence. For the most part, we acknowledge it and even belong to the church. But when God asserts a claim on us and asks of us love and faith, self, soul, and body, when God humbles himself for love of us, our response is most generally the same. Politely, but nonetheless clearly, we tell God in every way we can: thank you, God, but really I have more important things on my mind.

The silence of unconcern is crueler than the silence of hatred; but there are also those who hate.

Not all would come and go indifferently. Crucifixion was far from a quick and merciful death; it was long, drawn-out, and slow. The victim might hang for days till at length he died of thirst or starvation. What would there be to hold a crowd that long?

But some will stay. The gospel says, ". . . then they sat down and kept watch over him" (Matt. 27:36). They were not all there out of indifference or curiosity. Some at, least, were there to guard, to keep watch, to make sure he did not escape, to make certain his disciples made no attempt to rescue him. They watched him; this was their moment of triumph.

Think back now over the events that lead up to this moment. Each of the Gospels tells us how, early in the story, Jesus offended certain people. He was too popular, and he didn't give the important people the respect they wanted. The scribes and Pharisees among others set out very early in his ministry to find a way to destroy him. Now they have found a way, and taken advantage of their opportunity.

But think how long they waited for that moment. Think how they must have watched him day after day before this day. They watched and listened, silently awaiting their chance. And for all their silent watching and listening they never saw who he was, never heard what he was saying.

We often think that we would be so much better Christians if only we could see Jesus face-to-face ourselves, and hear him speak directly to us. But look at those who were there. Why didn't they see? How could they have stood in the crowd and listened to the sermon on the mount, how could they have seen him heal the sick and feed the multitude, how, above all, could they have sat there on Calvary before the cross and heard him pray for forgiveness for his murderers, and yet not have heard God's love, or seen the meaning of it?

This is the silence of hatred, a silence most difficult for love to penetrate. But this, like the silence of unconcern and indifference, is based on self-centeredness, a mixture of self-interest and fear.

Those who come and go do not believe that this affects them. They can be silent because they have found that the best way to stay out of trouble is to avoid it, and this is not really their concern.

Those who stay have seen something more. There are other watchers, of course: the women and John. We will come to them later. But those in the foreground, who sit down disrespectfully, have understood that this man meant to change their lives. If his claim was not challenged, their position would be challenged, their authority cut away. If he went on, they would either be destroyed or, of necessity, become his disciples themselves. So they had watched him in the past, not to see what he did, not to hear what he said, but only to find an opportunity, a means of attack, a weapon to destroy him. They built up a wall of silence around themselves. Through this wall nothing could penetrate unless it served their purpose. No sight, no sound was welcome that didn't fit their plan.

And this is not something unusual; such a barrier is easily built and we ourselves do it often. We hear that a friend is sick and send a card. We might do more, but that would be inconvenient. We could go to visit; we could offer help; we could remember them in our prayers. But that's not part of the plan we have made for our lives. The thought of behaving differently seldom penetrates the wall of self.

How often does the knowledge of sorrow reach through: the awareness of hunger and violence, unemployment, homelessness, and prejudice at home and abroad? If we ourselves aren't suffering, how often do we remember that someone else is and that this "other" is the brother or sister for whom Christ died? The wall of silence protects us. Unthinkingly, from force of habit, we shut out the sounds that might upset our comfortable worlds.

But sometimes the line between hatred and indifference is very thin. Sometimes the only difference is that those who hate, see more deeply. In a sense they are nearer the truth, because they see that the security of their lives is threatened and they seek to save their lives from any who would interfere with their self-satisfied security. And yet, as the crowd ebbed away and the silence of Calvary grew deeper, some sense of the true meaning of the event did begin to come through, even to some who had been hostile or indifferent. Some, at least, would begin to hear, however uncertainly in the silence, the incarnate word.

So at the end, "When the centurion saw what had taken place, he praised God and said, 'Certainly this man was innocent.' And when all the crowds who had gathered there for this spectacle saw what had taken place, the Bible tells us that they returned home, beating their breasts" (Luke 23:47–48).

So there is an element of understanding here; it's not deep, not profound, but it's a beginning.

Clearly those who stayed to the end have heard more than those who went away. Whatever their reasons—the soldiers, because they were paid, the centurion to carry out an unpleasant duty, the authorities and others for all their various reasons—whatever their reasons for being there, what they had heard and seen had left its mark.

They had seen him suffering torture, pain, and thirst, and yet, throughout all of it, speaking of love and forgiveness and committing his spirit into his father's hands in perfect confidence.

Of course he had died, as the two thieves had died, as all people die, but they can no longer be coldly indifferent. What they had seen and heard, and heard more clearly in the final silence than in the initial noise, had been no ordinary dying. This man, in his dying, had proclaimed his righteousness so clearly that even the Roman soldiers whose job it was to do this frequently, even they have heard. Even the watching crowd has been moved to sorrow.

There are writers who have pondered the effect of this day on some of the principal actors: the centurion, Pontius Pilot, Barabbas. Some think that these events would have left an indelible mark on all who took part in them. There is little in the gospel record to support any such theories. Perhaps these people saw that there was an injustice done; surely Pilate knew that. Maybe they were moved to sorrow or admiration like the centurion and others. But how many times have any of us seen an injustice, felt indignation, been moved to sorrow, and let the events slip from our conscious memory?

If this event left a lasting mark on these people, we have no record of it. And we are not much different.

We, too, can leave our watch on Calvary moved to sorrow for our sins, realizing anew how much evil we do so easily, humbled and penitent. If so, this is good—but it is nowhere near enough. That much was seen by many of these bystanders who never, so far as we know, understood the meaning of this day.

If the disciples had seen and heard no more than this, they would have gone back to their fishing and never have written a gospel, the Good News, centered on this event. If the church learned no more than that from the cross, it would hardly have called this a *good* Friday, God's Friday. If there was nothing more to see than a good man unjustly tortured and crucified, bearing bravely a shameful death, one more example of human cruelty and human nobility, no one would long have remembered and noticed.

But the central figure of Calvary, the figure of Christ on the cross, is no mere object of pity to behold with sorrow. He has not come to this in defeat and failure. He has not come here because his enemies have won. No, this is the path marked out for him by his father and he has come to it in perfect obedience to that will.

He came into this world, not to avoid evil or deny its existence, but to beat it down into final defeat. And here, now, that has been done. The worst that we can do, the worst effects of sin—he has met them and conquered them. The figure of Calvary is a symbol of power and triumph and victory.

If we watch with him and let him speak in our silence, we will hear of that triumph.

✝

CHAPTER III

THE SILENCE OF
THE DISCIPLES

THOSE WHO HAD FOLLOWED JESUS up to Jerusalem from Galilee had done so with mixed motives.

They had left many things for Jesus's sake: homes and work and duty, family and friends and familiar surroundings. They had come to believe that this Jesus was the Messiah. They had seen his love for people demonstrated over and over again in word and action. Yet as they came toward Jerusalem they could still miss the meaning of his parables, they could still block out of their minds the things he told them of the suffering ahead. They could still quarrel over who would sit on either side of the Lord in his kingdom.

And the scene as they entered the city of Jerusalem must have given substance to their brightest dreams. It was all true. It was happening. Jesus was being accepted as Messiah. But the days went by and the crowds began to melt away. The cheering crowd that threw robes and branches before him on Palm Sunday dwindled down to the few disciples who ate with Jesus the Passover meal and went out with him to Gethsemane. Even of the chosen twelve, one was gone before the meal was over.

Of those who remained, even the three closest to him, Peter and James and John, those who had seen his glory on the Mount of Transfiguration, those who he now had asked especially to watch with him and pray,

even these cannot help him, but fall asleep. They had
said they would never deny him or forsake him. Peter
had sworn it with an oath, and said he would be faithful
even if all the others should fail. But he also failed.

They had good intentions. We all have good intentions. But "when push comes to shove" we don't push
very hard. When the soldiers came, the disciples made
only the smallest token gesture to defend him and then,
the gospel tells us, "All of them deserted him and fled"
(Mark 14:50).

It is true that Peter did later return and stand outside the place of judgment. But when he was accused
of being one of Jesus' followers, he denied it. He swore
he did not know him. And so it was that when Jesus
was tried and condemned, the silence of his friends
was more terrible than the shouts from the crowd of
"Crucify him!"

Those who knew him best, who had called him
"Master" and "Lord," now, in the hour of his trial,
denied him, and by their silence left him to be crucified.

There is, we have said, a silence that is proper in the
presence of God, and there is a silence that cries out to
be broken. The silence of the disciples at this moment
cries out to be broken.

The prophet Jeremiah had been mocked when
he spoke God's word to God's people, and Jeremiah

resolved to speak no more in God's name or make mention of God again. He would hold his peace at the sight of injustice, oppression, and wrong. He would be silent. "But," he discovered, "within me there is something like a burning fire shut up in my bones; I am weary with holding it in, and I cannot" (Jer. 20:9).

So it would be with the disciples at Pentecost. There is a time when we have such news that we can't contain it. There is a time when we know such joy that we can't keep it to ourselves, but need to call in family and friends to share the joy and celebrate. There is a time when the word of God can't be contained in our hearts and minds and must be, must be, told to others. That time would come for the disciples. The silence of the disciples would at last be broken, and once broken it would be broken forever.

After Pentecost nothing—not the threat of death, or torture, or persecution—would be strong enough to make them silent again. And their deaths would speak as loudly as their lives of the gospel of God.

But now they are silent. They are silent, not out of indifference or hatred, but out of fear.

Those who have walked beside Jesus, with whom he had shared his life, flee now in shameful silence. And this silence, too, is familiar. Which of us has not kept silent when there were words to be said: to those ignorant of Christ and his church, to those who mock and those who sneer, to those who criticize and those who condemn? A word might be said, but we prefer to avoid problems and we let it pass.

But if we keep silence others will speak. If Jesus's followers will not bear witness for him, others are ready enough to bear witness against him. And so they do. And we, by our silence, bear witness also: to the weakness of our faith and the smallness of our true concern.

Nor is it only before his enemies that we are silent. How many of us dare talk of faith even to our friends or invite a neighbor to church? Time and again we betray Jesus by silence when only a word needs to be said, and that word is wanted and would be welcomed: by the sick who need and want to be reminded of how Christ shares our suffering, by the sorrowful who need and want to be told of the hope the gospel gives us, by the lonely who need and want to be told that Jesus is with them always. We could speak that word of courage and strength, but often we remain silent instead.

So we bear witness, either by words or by silence, and our silence bears witness against our faith. Our silence creates a void that others will fill. But even if we lack words, we can speak by our actions. There's a text to remember that may come from Peter himself: "For it is God's will that by doing right you should silence the ignorance of the foolish" (1 Pet. 2:15).

Scholars will argue whether the epistle that bears Peter's name comes from Peter himself or a follower of his, but that phrase certainly comes from Peter's experience. He who had three times denied his savior knew the high price of silence. He would know that the critics and scorners could be put to silence best by a life that spoke without doubt or denial of the power and love of God.

There is a silence that is proper in the presence of God, and there is a silence that cries out to be broken. The silence of those we have considered thus far cries out to be broken. It can be broken by words, but also by actions. And it can be done.

The indifference can be pierced, the walls of selfishness can be broken down, the fears can be conquered. It is possible for any one of these to keep us from hearing the word of God, to surround us with such silence, such walls, such barriers that God's love cannot come in. But few people can make the wall so strong that the silence is total.

The centurion heard enough even through his professional indifference to be moved to admiration. The bystanders, some of them, heard enough to be moved to sorrow. But they were sorry for him, not for themselves.

On the way to Calvary, the gospel tells us, a company of people and of women followed Jesus and bewailed and lamented him. And Jesus turned to them and said: "Do not weep for me, but weep for yourselves and for your children" (Luke 23:28).

Sorrow is not enough. Sorrow that fails to see beyond the suffering of Jesus the cause of that suffering has no lasting value. Sorrow is wasted unless it sees the cause in us. The reactions of the soldiers and the centurion, the company of women, and the bystanders don't go deep enough. They see only the surface; there is no basis for anything more.

But the silence of the disciples, although they fled, although they denied him, has space for growth. They at least know what they have done. They know who it is who is suffering. More important still, they know, though yet only dimly, why. For them the story of Good Friday cannot end at the cross. Now it seems to have ended, but the three years of discipleship will far outweigh the three days of separation. Over and over Jesus had told them what it would mean to follow him. And he had told them, after all, why he had come into the world and what was bound to happen.

He said, "the Son of Man must be handed over to sinners, and be crucified . . ." (Luke 24:7).

He said, "The Son of Man must undergo great suffering, and be rejected by the elders, chief priests and scribes, and be killed . . ." (Luke 9:22).

He said: "If any want to become my followers, let them deny themselves and take up their cross daily and follow me . . ." (Luke 9:23).

By words, by parables, he had told them that his ministry must meet with rejection, that his life must encounter suffering and death, that only by these means could he accomplish the purpose for which he had come. And they had heard, but not understood.

Now they are silent—from fear, yes, but more than that. Now for the first time they have really heard what he said. It was true. He had meant it. He was the Messiah, and he was rejected by those to whom he came. In their silence they would hear his words again, and now, at last, begin to understand.

So in former times the prophets had spoken again and again of the inevitable judgment that must come on the failures of God's people, and they had not been heard. No one had listened. No one had listened until later, when it happened as the prophets had said. Then, when defeat put a stop to their pride, they had remembered the prophets' message and listened. When God had silenced every competing voice, then they had listened. Too late to avoid defeat, but not too late to repent, they remembered the prophets' words and Jesus's words and saw the meaning of the event.

We human beings do not learn easily. But where God's word is present there is always the possibility of learning. When at last we are silenced by events beyond our control or manage somehow to put aside our distractions and listen, the word is there. We can repent and hear.

The disciples' flight was shameful. Their silence cried out to be broken. But their defeat, their failure, provided the possibility of penitence, sorrow for their failure, the emptying out of self that gives room for the growth of the Spirit. They needed to move from sorrow for Jesus and what they had done to him and finally understand—and act on that understanding.

It can be a painful process. Peter, the leader in so many ways of the others, the boldest, the first to assert that he would never deny his Lord, was also the first to do so. He said, "I do not know this man you are talking about" (Mark 14:71). But his denial, his silence, led him to a realization of his weakness and his need for the savior. The time came when "Peter remembered that Jesus had said to him, 'Before the cock crows twice, you will deny me three times.' And he broke down and wept" (Mark 14:72).

If we remember our times of silence, we might weep ourselves, but also, like Peter, see who we are and let God work in us as in Peter to begin again.

✝

CHAPTER IV

THE SILENCE
OF MARY

THE DISCIPLES HAD FLED.

Some commentators have speculated on what might have happened if they had not. Suppose Peter had made good his promise and stayed beside his Lord. He, too, might have been arrested; they might have bound him to Jesus, the disciple tied to his master, and he might have shared Jesus's death. What a theme that would make for meditation.

But there was one at the cross who was bound to him by cords stronger than those the soldiers used. We're not told that Mary followed him. We're not told what she said or thought. In fact, in all the gospels there is only a passing reference here and there to the mother of Jesus. How did she happen to be in Jerusalem? It wasn't her home; she couldn't have followed her son day by day in his travels.[1] Apparently that was unusual. Mark's Gospel tells us that she had "come up with him," but where was she at the triumphal entry, or during those last days, or at the time of the last supper? No Gospel tells us that. But at the cross, she was there (Mark 15:41).

Perhaps no one on Calvary could know the full meaning of what was done until later.

---

1. See, for example, Mark 3:31–35, Matthew 12:46–50, and Luke 8:19–21 where it is noted that Jesus's mother and brothers are outside.

That smallest group before the cross, unnoticed at first, and noticed now only in contrast to the absence of others, saw more fully than others how to respond and they did the only thing they could do: they watched. Mary, John, and some other women stood far off, watching in silence.

Only toward the end do the Gospels mention them. It's as if they had been concealed at first by the crowd or couldn't come near until the end. The hatred of the rulers, the vigilance of the soldiers, would not in all likelihood extend to the women, and probably John was young enough to escape notice as a possible source of trouble. So now they could stand near enough to see and hear something of what takes place, watching in silence before the cross.

This had been their role throughout Jesus's ministry: to watch, to follow, to accept. Almost any other task would have been easier. Remember the words of Simeon when the infant Jesus was presented in the temple: "This child is destined for the falling and the rising of many in Israel, and to be a sign that will be opposed . . . and a sword will pierce your own soul too" (Luke 2:34–35). It had been made clear from the beginning.

But how much could Mary really have understood of those things that she was asked to do?

When the angel Gabriel announced to her that she was to be the mother of the Messiah, she was afraid (Luke 1:29). She could not have known the extent of the challenge or what it meant or what the end of the matter would be, but so great a role in God's plan could not be lightly assumed. This was a wonderful, but also fearful, thing that she was asked to do. Yet her reply was the only reply God ever asks of us: "Let it be to me according to your word" (Luke 1:38).

Let's stop here for a moment to ask what choice Mary had. The archangel simply announced what was to happen. Could Mary have said, "No"? Theoretically, yes, of course. Our God calls us to freedom. Anglican theologian H. R. McAdoo has written, "Liberty of choice is not only the determining element in moral actions but one part of the divine plan for tempering human souls. Without it, and if actions were pre-determined, there would be no meaning or aim in the spiritual life."[2] Jeremy Taylor wrote that "Liberty is the hand and fingers of the soul by which she picks and chooses; and if she gather flowers, she makes for herself a garland of immortality."[3]

---

2. H. R. McAdoo, *The Structure of Caroline Moral Theology* (London: Longmans, Green, 1949), 44.
3. Jeremy Taylor, *The Whole Works of the Right Rev. Jeremy Taylor, D.D.*, "Ductor Dubitantium," Books III and IV, Vol. 10 (London: Brown, Green, and Longmans, et al., 1855), 552.

Mary was free to say no. But God knew who Mary was and what her response would be. We have no record of Mary's childhood and growth, but we know from her response to the angel what God knew already: that she was one who sought to serve God and would freely accept God's will. When I need help with a task, I ask some people and not others. Whoever I ask is free to say no, but I will not ask someone likely to turn me down.

Jesus, of course, was called to something harder, and prayed in Gethsemane that it might be otherwise. He also, of course, was free to say, "No;" to attempt to escape from the soldiers and return to Galilee. But God had called him to make his life a full and perfect offering, and God's will was his also.

Maybe the folly of human pride is nowhere so clearly seen as in our usual response when God calls us down a road we had not chosen, into paths hard to travel. We haven't chosen it for ourselves; we would rather not go. Imagine pitting our understanding and wisdom against that of God the creator. Yet we protest, we complain, we look for a way out, as if we knew better than God how the lives God has given us should be spent. "But who indeed are you, a human being" Paul asked, "to argue with God? Will what is molded say to the one who molds it, 'Why have you made me like this?'" (Rom. 9:20).

Some would call this a counsel of despair. How can we place ourselves, our lives, our welfare, our families, all our plans so completely in another's hands? How could we give up our freedom that far? It is, in fact, a frightening, not an easy, thing. There is scripture for it: "It is," the Epistle to the Hebrews says, "a fearful thing to fall into the hands of the living God" (Heb. 10:31).

And yet more fearful, it has been said, to fall out of them. And can that happen? In the largest sense, no, of course not. The old hymn says the obvious: "He's got the whole world in his hands." But suppose that somehow those hands were not there and we could fall out of them. That would be fearful indeed.

There's a critical and difficult issue involved: how to reconcile God's omnipotence and human freedom. There are some who argue that the human role is simply to accept God's omnipotence, to say that we are destined for heaven or hell and have no freedom to decide. Others have argued strongly that human freedom is essential to God's purpose.

What safety is there for us either way? What kind of freedom would we have if left to our own devices? Freedom is a means to an end; the way by which we can grow and develop ourselves most fully, become most truly who we really are, who we potentially are, because what we are meant to be is God-given; the road by which to reach it is a road God shows us, and the strength to follow it is God's gift alone.

What freedom is there except in the service of the One "whose service is perfect freedom?" (Book of Common Prayer, 99).

A friend of mine recently moved to San Francisco, bringing with him the three large fans that had cooled his home in the Midwest. He had not been in his new home for more than a few days when he learned that he will never need them. He is perfectly free, or course, to unpack them and plug them in, but what would be the point? I am likewise free to show up at a baseball traning camp in Florida, but I learned long ago that my skills are not an asset on the baseball diamond. I can rail against the fate that makes my house fans useless or keeps me safely in the spectator seats at a ball game, but surely it is better to accept the fact that I am destined for other things and seek to understand and utilize the skills I have than to bemoan my lack of the skills I might prefer. We speak about "God-given skills" for a reason.

The Russian philosopher-theologian Nicholas Berdyaev has written on this theme: "Man's suffering is two-fold. He suffers from the trials that are sent him, from the blows which fate deals him, from death, illness, privations, treachery, solitude, disillusionment, and so on, and so on. And he suffers, too, from rebelling against suffering, from refusing to bear it and from cursing it. And there is another and bitterer kind of suffering. When man accepts suffering and recognizes that it has a meaning, the pain grows less, becomes more endurable, and a light begins to shine through it. Unenlightened suffering, the most terrible of all, is that which man does not accept, against which he rebels and feels vindictive. But when he accepts suffering as having a higher meaning, it regenerates him. . . . Suffering tracks our steps, even the happiest of us. There is only one way open to man, the way of light and regeneration—to accept suffering as the cross which everyone must bear, following the Crucified. This is the deepest mystery of Christianity and of Christian ethics. Suffering is bound up with sin and evil, just as death is—the last of man's trials. But it is also the way of redemption, of light and regeneration. Such is the Christian paradox with regard to suffering and it must be accepted and lived through."[4]

Mary, like all of us, was free to say no. But her reply to the angel shows the wisdom of God's choice: "Let it be to me according to your word" (Luke 1:38). The

---

4. Nicholas Berdyaev, *The Destiny of Man* (New York: Charles Scribner, 1937), 118–119.

words foreshadow the words of the son she would now bear: "Your will be done." Jesus taught his disciples to say it in the Lord's Prayer (Matt. 6:10) and prayed it himself in Gethsemane (Matt. 26:42).

We have many pictures and statues and representations of the mother and child, many famous and beautiful works of art, but is not the true glory of Mary, her true example, in two scenes: the first, in which she calmly and obediently accepts that hard duty to which God has called her, and the second, in which, at the end, she stands by the cross and in silent obedience accepts the will of God?

What does God ask of us? Here is the answer: it is not understanding that he asks. Mary could not have fully understood how God's purpose was to be fulfilled through her son. She did not understand the adoration of the shepherds or the things spoken of the Christ child, though she kept these things and pondered them in her heart (Luke 2:19).

When Jesus at age twelve stayed behind in the temple and spoke to his mother and Joseph of being about his father's business, she could not have understood (Luke 2:49). Nor did Mary know what Jesus would do at the wedding feast at Cana (John 2:1–11), nor did she understand when he set out to preach and to gather followers, nor did she understand when he turned to go up to Jerusalem in the face of growing opposition, hatred, and danger. When the body of Jesus was taken down from the cross and placed again in her arms, she could scarcely have understood why God should have called her to bring forth a son to meet this criminal's death. But it is not understanding that God asks.

Nor does God ask for our talents. How often we make that mistake. "I don't know enough to talk about religion with anybody." "I can't invite the neighbors to church with me; I know so little about the church myself."

Oh, but we all make that mistake. I'm bothered every year at the appeals sent out by our seminaries. We must support them, we are told, so we can have the best trained, best equipped, most talented clergy possible. Well, maybe. Yes, the seminaries do need our support, and we do need to give those who are called to the ministry the best support and training we can, but all God really needs is a voice and a pair of hands. It is God's word that needs to be spoken, God's love that needs to be shown to the world by the ministry of the church, and no one is talented enough for that; no training can adequately prepare us for that; but no one who depends on God can fail to do God's will.

So it is not our talents God asks. What witness could Mary bear for her son; what assistance could she offer him? All she should give him—but it is all God ever asks—was this: trust enough and love, humbly, obediently, unquestioningly to accept the will of God.

It would have been wonderful, we said, if Peter had stayed by his Lord, if he had been bound to him by the soldiers, perhaps if he had shared his death. So Mary was bound to him by a stronger tie. The body he had received from her—her flesh and blood—was suffering and dying.

And with her stood the disciple Jesus loved. The Gospel doesn't say it was John, but just "the one whom Jesus loved" (John 20:2). Some have speculated that John avoids his own name here for a reason. Throughout the story of the Passion and the Resurrection John uses that longer, more awkward phrase, and some say he does it to make of himself a symbol of every disciple, of all who would be disciples—disciples Jesus loves.

Maybe he means to say that we, too, if we could, would have stood there; that we, too, belong at the foot of the cross. And we do belong there. Tied to him by bonds stronger than rope and links of iron, we have been made members of his body by baptism, sharers of his life, of his own body and blood, in the sacrament of the altar. "Rejoice," says the Epistle of Peter, "insofar as you are sharing Christ's sufferings" (1 Pet. 4:13).

The sacraments we receive are the evidence that we are joined to him, the means by which we are united with him in his own body, sharers in the church of one common life. And we may know something like Mary's sorrow, that it is not some other life poured out here, but our own.

In silence before the cross stood Mary, the beloved disciple, and the other women. There were things that might have been said, questions that might have been asked, but we have no record of them. We know only this: that they stood there in silence, watching, waiting, trusting that even in this, somehow, God's will would be done.

They might have asked what would become of them now, now that they have given up everything to follow Christ only to see him crucified. They might have asked many things, but there was no need to ask. Jesus had said, "Your Father knows what you need before you ask" (Matt. 6:8), and he who served his father perfectly also knows the needs of his followers before they ask. So he breaks the silence to provide for them: "Woman, here is your son . . . Here is your mother" (John 19:26–27). The care and protection that he can no longer give them himself, he gives them in each other.

So he had always seen the needs of others and provided for them before he was asked. So he had seen the need of the five thousand and fed them, knowing their hunger (Matt. 14:21 and others). So, often, he had reached out to forgive and to heal without being asked, even though the throng and his own disciples might try to keep the needy from him. And so he knows all our needs, our real needs, better than we do and provides for them.

He had often in his ministry rebuked those who make long speeches and prayers. He was never concerned with elegant speeches and elaborate words. The best prayer always is the prayer of silence, a humble and obedient waiting on God. That prayer is always answered. To the silent heart, God will speak.

There were hundreds of people who passed by the cross that day, and countless words that were spoken. Yet in paintings and statues there are only two figures traditionally shown: Mary and John, the mother of Christ and the beloved disciple, those who followed in silence.

✝

CHAPTER V

THE SILENCE
OF JESUS

THE SILENCE OF CALVARY is broken by the noise of the soldiers casting lots, finding some amusement and distraction in the midst of an unpleasant duty. The silence is broken by the dying cries of the prisoners, by the officials, by the crowd. In the general confusion of sound the silence of John and the women goes almost unnoticed.

But above the scene is one figure whose silence slowly quiets all the rest. The tumult of the crowd dies down because they have done all they can. The rulers, the soldiers, the watchers can do nothing now but wait in silence. And his followers are silent through fear and helplessness. There is nothing they can do either.

Nothing more can be done. All that can be done is being done in silence by the bleeding, dying figure on the cross. More and more clearly as the day wears on, he is not the victim but the victor; the initiative is in his hands though they are nailed and broken. He alone of all those on Calvary is acting. He is offering the Father all that is needed for the healing of the world. Nailed to the cross, the victim of pride and indifference, of every weakness and human sin, still he is the conqueror. In these last hours he brings to perfect completion the work he had come into the world to do.

How much oratory and effort has been spent since the world began in trying to make people good, to

conquer sin and evil, to improve the human race. You
know the familiar phrases and slogans. Some speak of it
as "human betterment," others as "social progress." Some
call it one thing, some another. It has been identified
with the Roman Empire, with feudalism, with commu-
nism, nationalism, Americanism, capitalism, democ-
racy. Whatever the prescription, and some, of course,
are better than others, still all are imperfect, they arise
from recognition of the presence in the world of evil, of
sin, and the need to control or remedy those evils.

Human beings have often wanted to change their
world and their lives and the lives of others for the
better. Countless human beings, good and bad, have
spent themselves in words or deeds to cure the sick-
ness. But here once and for all, it is done, though his
hands and feet are nailed and bleeding, though he has
scarcely strength enough to speak those few words that
are needed.

It is, we have said, silent, loving obedience that God
wants most of all, and in Christ Jesus that obedience is
most perfectly given, God's work is most perfectly done.
And he who said, "Not my will but yours be done," can
also say, "It is finished. . . . Into your hands I commend my spirit" (John 19:30, Luke 23:46).

Never did he have any other will than his Father's;
never did he speak or act in any other name. His spirit

has always been in his Father's hands. No more was needed. No more is ever needed. It is a simple thing, but a hard lesson for each of us to learn.

A story is told of Samuel Isaac Joseph Schereschewsky, bishop of Shanghai in the late nineteenth century, who was an invalid during the last third of his life, and yet in that time translated the whole of the Bible into a Chinese dialect. He was so paralyzed that he could only use one finger to work with, and he typed the whole two thousand pages with the middle finger of his partially crippled right hand. His spirit is best expressed in words spoken four years before his death: "I have sat in this chair," he said, "for over twenty years. It seemed very hard at first, but God knew best. He kept me for the work for which I am best fitted."

To question and challenge is a natural human response, but what cannot be changed can often be used constructively with God's help. All that is needed is the quiet turning to God that is the material of saints.

Perhaps we fail to notice enough the silence of Christ. We remember his words, his parables, his sermons. It was said of them that "never has anyone spoken like this" (John 7:46). Constantly the crowds followed him to hear his words; seldom could he escape from them for periods of silence and prayer. They followed and listened. They saw him debate those who came with questions. In all that he had no equal. Try as they would to catch him or trick him with problems and questions, it was always the questioners who came away defeated, unable to answer his questions or to hide their confusion. At last they gave up the useless effort, and the Gospel tells us, "No one was able to give him an answer, nor from that day did anyone dare to ask him any more questions" (Matt. 22:46).

"Never has anyone spoken like this." And yet from the beginning he was also a man of silence.

Forty days of silence marked the beginning of his ministry, and time and again through his three years of public ministry he withdrew from the crowd, left his disciples alone, and went off by himself in silence. Now, at the end of his ministry, the silence grows deeper.

Each day of the last week he had withdrawn from the city at night to rest and pray. At the last supper he told them, "I will no longer talk much with you" (John 14:30). Now the words that needed to be said had been spoken, the actions had been taken, he had made his witness to the truth. Now others must decide.

"Then the high priest stood up before them and asked Jesus, 'Have you no answer? What is it that they testify against you?' But he was silent and did not answer" (Mark 14:60–61).

"Pilate asked him again, 'Have you no answer? See how many charges they bring against you.' But Jesus made no further reply, so that Pilate was amazed" (Mark 15:4–5).

It was as the Prophet Isaiah had written: "He was oppressed, and he was afflicted, yet he did not open his mouth; like a lamb that is led to the slaughter, and like a sheep that before its shearers is silent, so he did not open his mouth" (Isa. 53:7).

For now there is nothing to say. They accuse him of claiming to be the Messiah, yet he never laid claim to that title. He was, in truth, the Messiah, but when others pressed the title on him, he commanded them to be silent. When the time had come to ask his disciples for their judgment of him, their understanding of who he was, he led them out of the city on a quiet country road, and asked them, "Who do people say that I am?" and receiving their answers, he asked, "But who do you say that I am?" Peter answered him, 'You are the Messiah.' And he sternly ordered them not to tell anyone about him" (Mark 8:30).

If others will acknowledge him, it must be for what others see him to be, not for what he claims for himself. So even now he will make no claim for himself. He had said, "If I glorify myself, my glory is nothing. It is my father who glorifies me" (John 8:54). Silence is the only answer he can give to the repeated demand of Pilate and the chief priest and the elders that he answer their questions and their charges. Only those who seek the truth can be given it.

To the point blank question, "Are you the king of the Jews?" the only reply is, "You say so" (Luke 23:2). What value do words have? They are human devices. Like any human device they can be twisted and used however we wish. Metal can be made into a plow or a sword. Words can be used to praise or condemn. They are like empty containers to be filled with any meaning we choose. "Are you the Messiah?"

"The words are yours; you may use them if you like; I am who I am." Those who desire the truth will receive it.

"Pilate asked him, 'So you are a king?' Jesus answered, 'You say that I am a king. For this I was born, and for this I came into the world, to testify to the truth. Everyone who belongs to the truth listens to my voice.' Pilate asked him, 'What is truth?'" (John 18:38).

These various people, Pilate, the chief priests, the elders, are not concerned with truth. The rulers are concerned with putting down a threat to their positions; Pilate is concerned with keeping the peace and preventing disorder. The people are concerned with having their will carried out. Truth is a minor concern for all of them.

They had seen Christ heal the sick. They had heard his teaching. He had freely spoken with them and answered their questions. If their eyes and ears had been open to the truth, they could have heard it and seen it. But their minds were not open; they were closed and stopped. When they saw people healed, they condemned him for breaking the Sabbath. When they heard him speak, they listened only to those words that pleased them and chose not to remember the words that did not. When they asked him questions, they sought only to trip and confuse him. The truth did not interest them.

At his trial, they sought only some evidence to use against him, some pretext for new charges and accusations. Blinded by jealousy, deafened by self-concern, they had made up their minds, and now they wanted only some evidence, some legal grounds, for proceeding as they had planned to proceed. You have perhaps seen the slogan that says: "Don't bother me with the facts; my mind is made up." Put that way we see the foolishness of it, but that is a common attitude of which we are probably all guilty sometimes. We form snap judgments and stick with them. Every bit of evidence to back us up, counts double. The contrary evidence— well, that's the exception that proves the rule.

And nowhere is this more evident than in politics and religion. All we need is a label: Democrat or

Republican, fascist or communist, high church or low church. The facts don't matter; the meaning of the labels doesn't matter; the values involved don't need to be weighed. All we need is a label to save us from having to think.

So a political party with an appealing candidate tends to leave the party label off the campaign posters to make people use some other basis of judgment, even, perhaps, the facts and the issues. If the candidate is a poor one, on the other hand, the party label is there.

So, too, in matters of religion, we find it easier to stay on a familiar path, to do things the familiar way, and especially if we don't know the reason for it. We might find new ways of prayer, a new and deeper meaning in the Bible, new ways to serve God in our daily lives. We might really begin to grow in God's service. But it's always easier to stay inside our familiar walls, our usual ruts, and keep ourselves as safe as a coffin in the grave.

Truth is dangerous. Truth is upsetting. Truth makes no allowances for personal preference or comfort. But truth is of God. And without the truth how can we bear witness to him? What can we say of Christ? Have we seen him and known him and heard his words? Or are we also afraid that if we listened and heard his truth, we would know his claim on our lives?

Before his accusers, Jesus is silent. They will not hear the truth or acknowledge his claim. Yet his very silence must call to mind the words of the prophet Isaiah. His accusers must see that his patience and silence and suffering proclaim who he is as loudly and clearly as his healing acts and his sermons. Their hatred cannot silence that silent Word, that proclamation. Nailed to the cross, he needs no title above his head. Pilate had caused one to be placed there as the accusation of a criminal generally was put on a placard for the world to read. And Pilate had worded it deliberately to mock his accusers: "THIS IS JESUS, THE KING OF THE JEWS."

And mock them it does. They went to Pilate and asked him to change it so it would read, "This man said, I am King of the Jews" (John 19:21). But Pilate had yielded to pressure enough for one day, and he refused their request. It's a foolish battle they fight. Christ proclaims more loudly than any title or sign, by the sign of his patient suffering, by his love, by his offering of himself, by his silent witness—by all these he proclaims who he is.

"Never has anyone spoken like this!" (John 7:46). That was the reply of the soldiers sent early in his ministry to arrest him and bring him before the rulers for a hearing. Thus they were defeated in their first attempt to seize him by his eloquence. They sought stronger means. But even his silence defeats them. He has answered all their charges with the silence they deserve and silenced them by his silence.

Now from the cross he continues to speak as no one ever spoke before, by words, indeed, when words are needed, but above all by silence.

> Sev'n times he spake, sev'n words of love;
>> And all three hours his silence cried
> For mercy on the souls of men . . .

The words of the hymn may be familiar, but they serve only to emphasize that long silence. And the first word reminds us how that silence is being used: "Father, forgive them, for they know not what they do." He has no answer for the jeers of the crowd or the insults. Perhaps he has not even heard them. The silence of Jesus is eloquent witness that his thoughts, his prayers, his whole attention, are turned, as they have always been, to God. The phrase, "He was not so much a man of prayer as prayer itself" was never more evident than here. It is not words that he offers, but himself for us. He is himself the world's most perfect prayer, its most selfless offering.

In the silence he makes that offering, and the first and the last words from the cross frame that silence:

"Father, forgive them" (Luke 23:34). "Father, into your hands" (Luke 23:46).

Each word, each break in the silence, comes almost by accident, as if unconsciously the words had slipped out from his silent meditation, his concentration on the Father's will.

✝

CHAPTER VI

THE SILENCE
OF GOD

Each word, each break in the silence, comes almost by accident, as if unconsciously the words had slipped out from his silent meditation, his concentration on the Father's will.

So it is still at that darkest moment of Calvary when we move beyond the silence of the crowd and the silence of the disciples to a deeper silence. For beyond all human silence is the silence indicated by that word from the cross: "My God, my God, why have you forsaken me?" (Matt. 27:46).

There are words of Jesus from an earlier time in his ministry that seem in striking contrast to these. At the tomb of Lazarus it is recorded that Jesus said, "Father, I thank you for having heard me. I knew that you always hear me, but I have said this for the sake of the crowd standing here, so that they may believe that you sent me" (John 11:41–42).

"I knew that you always hear me. . . ." In him are most perfectly united both human being and God, yet now, in this moment of deepest suffering, God seems silent. Jesus has given his life to the Father. His will has always been subject to the Father's will. "My food," he said, "is to do the will of [the one] who sent me" (John 4:34).

Even the words he spoke, he said, were not his words, but the words the Father had given him. Now there is no word, only silence, and Jesus, whose life had been itself one great offering of prayer, hears no answer, feels God to be absent, and yet still prays in the familiar words of the psalm: "My God . . . why have you forsaken me?"

It is only with the greatest difficulty that we can come into this silence. The spiritual experience out of which these words come is far beyond ours, not because Jesus is God, but because even his human nature is so much fuller than ours.

All of us pray at times; perhaps we pray regularly, and all of us have known in our prayer a feeling of futility, the feeling not only that our prayers were not answered, but perhaps even beyond that, the feeling that our prayers were not heard. But that hardly means that we have shared this experience of Jesus. For most of us, maybe for all of us, the feeling of dryness in our prayer, the sense that somehow the lines of communication have been broken or never established, comes, I think, from our inexperience. We are too often too deeply involved in other things.

Our whole life is far from being bound up in prayer, and our dryness in prayer is often experienced just at those times when we try to pray a little better—and suddenly realize what total amateurs we are.

These words of Jesus come from a deeper level by far, from the agony of a soul cut off from the one thing that matters, a soul that has always sought only to be in God's presence, to hear the Father's words, to be turned toward God not only in formal moments of prayer but in each act, each thought, each breath. Prayer for Jesus was no occasional activity, but life itself. He could say confidently, "I knew that you always hear me" (John 11:42). Now, on the cross, this confidence is gone. Beyond the physical suffering comes a spiritual suffering far deeper and more intense, the agony of desolation in which he seems to be cut off not only from other human beings, his followers, his disciples, but even, worst of all, from God.

How this could be, no one can say; why it should be, I think we can have some understanding.

Jesus had come to share all our experience, to take up into himself all the pain, all the sorrow, all the evil. To complete this work, it was necessary to drink this cup and know all its bitterness, and not as one who can say, "This too will pass; I can do this confident of a brighter tomorrow," but as one who shares all our weakness, and cannot see the end or the reason, who cannot see why God should command this thing, who cannot even see the presence of God in it—and yet will follow where God calls.

The author of the Epistle to the Hebrews says, ". . . we do see Jesus, who for a little while was made lower than the angels, now crowned with glory and honor because of the suffering of death, so that by the grace of God he might taste death for everyone. It was fitting that God, for whom and through whom all things exist, in bringing many children to glory, should make the pioneer of their salvation perfect through sufferings" (Heb. 2:9–10).

And the author of the Epistle to the Hebrews goes on to say that it is this very thing that enables us to pray with confidence, to go to Jesus in need and suffering, just because he has known every human temptation and trial. He knows because he has been there. This is how he is made perfect, complete, as our mediator, redeemer, and advocate: by sharing this deepest of all human pain: when prayer itself seems unheard, when God seems to have left us alone, when even hope seems vain. John of the Cross, a great spiritual teacher of the sixteenth century called it "the dark night of the soul."

It is not, perhaps, on the same level as our own experience of prayer, but it is a note that appears in the experience of those who have listened most closely to God. One might say that this deepest sense of abandonment is reserved for those who have loved God most: that silence, that desolation, that sense or feeling that God no longer hears. And this experience is reflected in the Psalms, which both express and shape so much of the spiritual knowledge of God's people.

The words that slip out from our Lord in this agony are the words of Psalm 22, and the opening verses of that psalm speak of this sense of desolation:

> Oh my God, I cry by day,
> but you do not answer,
> and by night, but find no rest. (Ps. 22)

The words of Psalm 13 express the same experience:

> How long, O Lord? Will you forget me forever?
> How long will you hide your face from me?
>
> (Ps. 13:1)

And there are similar passages in Psalms 10, and 42, and 43. It is common to have doubts. It is common to be uncertain and lose confidence. Those who have really prayed have invariably known this experience. In our own lesser way, maybe we've known it too. Prayer is not a magic formula; there's no recipe that will always work: no sincerity, devotion, constancy, in any proportion that permits us to gain control of God or open up a path of infallible access. Prayer's effectiveness can never be measured by the amount of change it accomplishes, or the degree to which we can sense God's presence.

But we do want to know we are heard, don't we? Sometimes you'll see prayers that go something like this:

O God, help us to know and to feel your presence . . .

or

O God, make us aware of your help. . . .

Well, certainly the feeling of God's presence, the awareness of God's love, the sense that God is with us is nice to have, and could be a wonderful help and strength. But I think we need to avoid the temptation to give up on prayer or our attendance at church or reading of the Bible, to excuse ourselves from it, because we're so conceited as to think that God really does not hear us simply because we don't hear God, don't feel God's presence. Sometimes people say they gave up because they "didn't get much out of it." That's pride for you: to judge truth by the test of our own senses and feelings.

We live in a scientific age. We ought to learn a lesson from scientists about the amount of trust we can place in our own senses and feelings. Bacteria and viruses do exist whether or not we can see them. The earth still curves no matter how flat it may seem. The seemingly solid wall is made up of moving atoms. Stars scarcely visible to our eyes are in fact larger than the earth and the sun and planets. We should know by now how little our senses can tell us about reality.

It is faith, not the senses, that gives the psalmist confidence to pray still to the God who is felt to be absent, whose answer the psalmist cannot hear:

> Why are you so cast down, O my soul,
>> and why are you so disquieted within me?
> Hope in God, for I shall again praise him . . .
>
>> (Ps. 43:5)

So, also, the other psalms of complaint and desolation move on to an affirmation of faith in God, a faith without which there would not be one to whom to make a complaint. So Psalm 22, the first words of which were overheard by the watchers at Calvary, moves on also to a hymn of praise:

> I will tell of your name to my brothers and sisters;
> in the midst of the congregation I will praise
>> you. . . .
> For he did not despise or abhor the affliction
>> of the afflicted;
> he did not hide his face from me,
> but heard when I cried to him. (Ps. 22:22, 24)

And think also about this: is it, do you think, a bit strange to find our Lord, the teacher of prayer, the man of prayer, quoting a psalm, using someone else's prayer on the cross?

Maybe we can learn something from this also. There is in the Bible and in the Book of Common Prayer something that will reflect every mood, every situation, every sorrow, every joy. These, coming as they do from centuries of human experience, sum up all that God has revealed to us of God and all the ways human beings have found to express their longing for God and to express God's praise.

If we make use of this treasure, enter into this great inheritance, we will find ourselves quite naturally selecting and choosing those prayers, those sentences, that most nearly express our own understandings. And that's good. But if we look further, we will find more than self-expression here. We will also find better ways and deeper experience. What is here has been proved and tested by generations before us. And because that is so, we will find that it leads us on from our own limitations, and that it will balance our partial insights with fuller understanding. The great value of the prayer book and Bible is that they make us keep a balanced diet. They correct our all-too-frequent mistakes and misunderstandings. If we want to complain against God, if we hear no answer to our prayer, there are words to express that attitude. But they don't simply reflect. They don't merely express our complaints for us and leave us there. Rather, they lead us on to acts of faith and trust and finally to hymns of praise.

So it was that Psalm 22 reflected Jesus's own sense of desolation. But in that terrible silence it also gave him words to say to the Father that led him on to words of praise so that at the end he could say with perfect trust: "Father, into your hands I commend my spirit."

And in our prayer and our moments of sorrow and isolation we can do the same. Though God is silent to the human senses, though we feel forsaken and abandoned, though we have doubts and uncertainties, it is still to God we must make our prayer and it is from God we will receive all the help we need.

Still in the silence, Jesus prays, trusting beyond understanding and knowledge, beyond logic and sense. Through such faith he comes to his triumph, and to share in this triumph we must have faith enough to follow him even into this deepest silence of all.

✝

CHAPTER VII

THE SILENCE
OF THE TOMB

They took his body down from the cross and sealed it in the tomb. There it would stay until the third day. The light had been put out. St. John says in one terrible verse:

> And this is the judgment, that the light has come into the world, and people loved darkness rather than light because their deeds were evil. (John 3:19)

It is then our own choosing that brings us into this deepest darkness and the silence of the tomb.

Jesus said he had come to show people the light and the truth, but the light does not always show us what we want to see and the truth does not always tell us what we want to hear. We would like to be told all is well with us, that a few minor adjustments may be indicated, but the patient is in no great danger. And if that is what we want to hear, there's always someone around who will gladly say it to please us.

Some Christian saints have said that when we die, we will first of all come face-to-face with Jesus. That would be light and truth enough; but could we face that light? A bishop I knew years ago would say that he thought he might rather be fried. To come face to face with Jesus and remember how we have lived . . . might it not be more comfortable to go elsewhere?

But in this world, in this present time, we need not face such light. We can turn aside from the light, we can shut our eyes and our ears. And if worst comes to worst, we can put the light out.

That is what other people like you and me did on Calvary:

[they] rolled a great stone to the door of the tomb and went away. (Matt. 27:60)

The darkness of the sky over all the earth for those last three hours cannot compare with the darkness of the three days that followed. The light is put out. The word of God is silent.

The Word that the world would not receive has been silenced by human sin. We have created the silence of the tomb. Our sins have silenced God. The voice that spoke God's love is silent because we willed that it should be. And in our lives, because we will it, the voice of God is silent.

Or so it seems. In fact, of course, it is our own lack of silence that keeps us from hearing. Our own words, our own faults, our own desires, our own will—where these have the upper hand, what room is left for God's Word in our souls?

They put him to silence by leaving no silence in which he might be heard—and so do we. It is not only our normal lives that are too full, too unquiet, though that is bad enough, but the places reserved for silence seem also to be filled with so much business and noise that if it were not done in God's name and clearly labeled "church work," God might well suspect that we were trying to silence God even in God's own house. Sometimes our parish calendars are so filled with meetings and conferences and projects and plans that one might well wonder where the time will come from to find out God's will for us in all these things.

We will, of course, refer briefly to God at the beginning of our meetings, and perhaps at the end if we remember. But how much in between is really done in God's name and to God's glory? But we can go further than that and ask: In the quietest part of our lives, in our own private prayers, how much silence is there really?

> The LORD is in his holy temple, let all the earth keep silence before [God]. (Hab. 2:20)

When we enter God's presence with our daily prayers, how much silence do we keep? I can speak for myself. Isn't it a fact that our prayers are often so filled with our own desires and hopes and petitions and accomplishments, a list of thanksgivings, confessions, and petitions, that we can spend the whole time of prayer looking not upward but inward? Surely God wants all these. There is no part of our lives God does not want; no interest of ours that does not concern God. But is that all? Where in all this is the silence in which God can give us the best gift of all?

We would not think of it; we could not imagine it; we cannot deserve it; but if we give God our silence, God has promised to place within us God's Living Word, God's own Son.

There was so little silence that week in Jerusalem, a typical city at a typically busy time. There was so little silence at the cross. Small wonder they failed to hear.

But what about us? Can we also fail to hear the Word of God sent among us, the Word of God nailed up for us to see? We know, if we are honest with ourselves, that we are no different from the various men and women who were there, who kept their various silences before the cross. We know that in each of us are those elements that are silent from hatred, silent from fear, from shame, from doubt, from business with other things.

The silence of the tomb is a man-made silence. We can and do create the silence in ourselves and around ourselves often and again. We take sins so lightly; we forget them so easily; we let them pass so quickly that it never occurs to us that somewhere they may carry weight and we should weigh them before we let them go.

Perhaps we will not forget so easily if we see the weight God puts on them. So here is the weight God gives them: the weight of our sins is the weight of the rock that sealed the Word of God in the tomb. That silence, when we think of it, may remind us what silence can be.

The church on Good Friday also has the darkness of the tomb. Its beauty is taken away and we create the silence within it for a purpose. But sometimes on other days as well, the church, for all its usual beauty and color, is still a tomb in which the Word of God is sealed as surely as if a rock were rolled across the door. This rock, also, is our creation, but we will find we can place it there or move it easily according to our will.

Our church, the Christian community of which we are a part, will speak of Christ or conceal him according to the choices we make. We will find, nevertheless, that however we may reveal or conceal our Lord in our church life and private lives, the Word of God cannot be kept in the tomb by our will. We may be silent, but not God's Word. Church doors and church walls can no more close in that Word than the cross or the tomb or our sin.

This tomb, you see, is not like other tombs. Christ once compared the Pharisees to whitewashed tombs, painted and planted with flowers on the outside but containing only dust and ashes within (Matt. 23:27).

This tomb is not like that. This tomb, though dead to all outward appearance, contains life.

Jesus had spoken of how a seed, so long as it continues alone, can do nothing, but if it falls to the ground and dies, it will bear fruit. So the seed has fallen and lies germinating within the ground.

The silence of this tomb is not that of death but of life. God does not resist or override our will, but the silence of human beings, the silence of God's Word, the silence of the tomb is not, could never be, the end of the matter.

There is a time to keep silence and a time to speak. There is a silence that is proper in God's presence and a silence that cries out to be broken. So the silence of the tomb must be broken, for God's word must be made known and God's truth revealed. The psalm says:

Our God comes, and does not keep silence . . .
(Ps. 50:3)

When, at the beginning of Holy Week, Jesus and his followers came up the road from Jericho and approached the walls of Jerusalem, St. Luke tells us that:

As he was now approaching the path down from the Mount of Olives, the whole multitude of the disciples began to praise God joyfully with a loud voice

for all the deeds of power that they had seen, saying, "Blessed is the king who comes in the name of
the Lord! Peace in heaven, and glory in the highest
heaven!" Some of the Pharisees in the crowd said
to him, "Teacher, order your disciples to stop." He
answered, "I tell you, if these were silent, the stones
would shout out." (Luke 19:37–40)

God will not be left without witnesses in the world
whatever the barriers may be.

Our God comes and does not keep silence,

before him is a devouring fire,

and a mighty tempest all around him. (Ps. 50:3)

Hear, O my people, and I will speak . . .

(Ps. 50:7)

The heavens proclaim his righteousness . . .

(Ps. 97:6)

If human beings are silent, God will speak. The creation itself will speak of its creator.

So at Jesus's death, in that deepest silence, the
stones did cry out, the earth did quake, and the rocks
were torn apart. Death, through human beings, has its
brief victory over the Lord of life, and nature trembles.

The creation itself bears witness. And how often have wood and stone borne better witness than we? One of the psalms contains an old Hebrew riddle which, in its original form, probably went something like this: "What has neither speech or language, but yet makes its voice heard in all the world?"

The answer is: "The heavens are telling the glory of God, and the firmament proclaims [God's] handiwork" (Ps. 19:1).

Heaven and earth, wood and stone, can bear witness to God in silence, and often better witness than our own. And wood and stone can be shaped to make a cross, to build a church to shelter God's people, to show Christ crucified and Christ triumphant.

But work at it as we will, how hard it is to shape our lives to look like his. How hard it is to shape and form them to bear his likeness. We are such poor material to work with and we have so little patience for God's forming hand.

Yet the bodies we bear were created in the image of God. They are, in origin, an expression of God's own being. They have no other purpose than to speak of God, to express, by the lives we lead, God's worship and praise. Nailed to the cross with him, they can do just that. If we will die with him, we may also rise again and share with him that life beyond the silence of the tomb, which is to praise God forever.